CONDUCTING BUSINESS WITH CHINA

Conducting Business With China

IS IT GOOD BUSINESS OR POOR MANAGEMENT?

Dr. Peter J. Tsivitse

Copyright © 2017 Dr. Peter J. Tsivitse
All rights reserved.

ISBN: 1541092627
ISBN 13: 9781541092624

This book is dedicated to my wife, Marilyn.
So she knows how much I appreciate her unending patience with listening to my stories about business and China.

Contents

  Map of China · ix

  Foreword · xi

  Preface · xv

Part One: Background Information · 1

Chapter 1 Introduction · 3

Chapter 2 The Path to Loss · 6

Part Two: Case Studies and Testimony · · · · · · · · · · · · · · · · · · 9

Chapter 3 Case # 1 - The Start · · · · · · · · · · · · · · · · · · · 11

Chapter 4 Case #2 - A Big Project · · · · · · · · · · · · · · · · · 12

Chapter 5 Case # 3 - Electric Motor Outsourcing · · · · · · · · · · · · 16

Chapter 6 Case #4 - Small Motor Manufacture · · · · · · · · · · · · · · 20

Chapter 7 Case #5 - An Opportunity · · · · · · · · · · · · · · · · · · · 22

Chapter 8 Case #6 - General Electric Korea · · · · · · · · · · · · · · · 24

Chapter 9 Case # 7 - China Survey · 26

Chapter 10 Case #8 - The Communications Venture · · · · · · · · · · · · 28

Chapter 11 Case #9 - The Pool Motor · 34

Chapter 12 Case #10 - American Superconductor Company (AMSC) · · 36

Chapter 13 Case #11 - The Electric Lawn Mower · · · · · · · · · · · · · · · 39

Chapter 14 Case #12 - The Electric Car · 41

Chapter 15 Case #13 The German Way · 45

Chapter 16 Case #14 The Electric Truck · 48

Chapter 17 Case #15 International Trade · 51

Chapter 18 Japan, Inc. · 55

Part Three: Conclusions and the Future · 59

Chapter 19 Business Leadership · 61

Chapter 20 American Imperialism · 63

Chapter 21 The Fundamentals · 68

Chapter 22 The Future · 71

Chapter 23 Conclusion · 75

       Acknowledgements · 79

       About the Author · 81

       Notes · **83**

Figure 3. China: Special Economic Zones

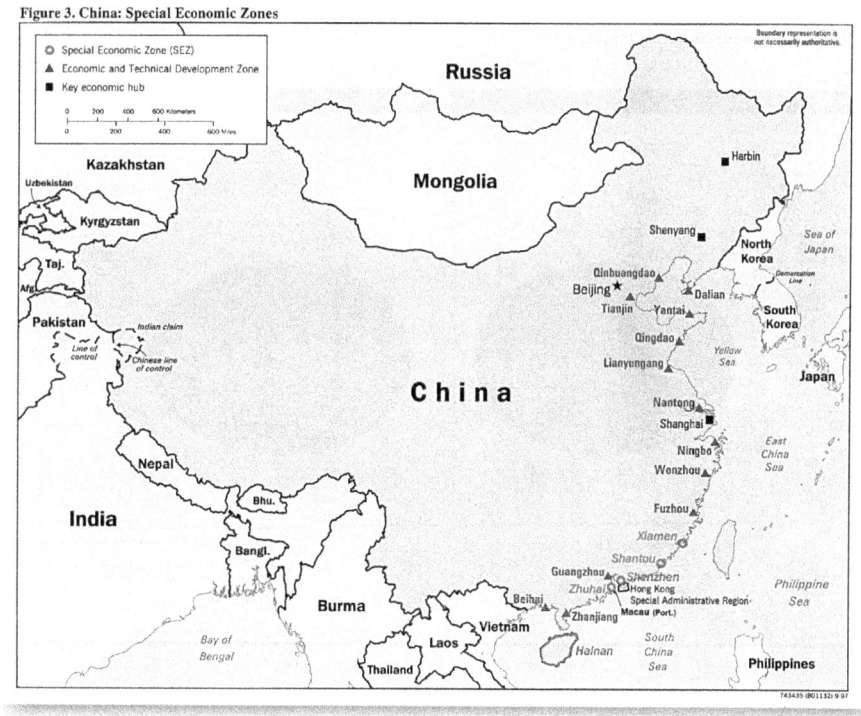

Foreword

I was first introduced to Pete Tsivitse by Chuck Ames, former CEO of Reliance Electric Company and an advisor/investor with our private equity firm, CapitalWorks, LLC. We were planning to purchase a specialty electric motors business in Indiana and were looking for board members with strategic connections and deep knowledge of the industry. Pete had spent his entire career with Reliance, beginning in engineering, then in engineering management, then in operating management and ultimately on the company's senior leadership team as Corporate Vice President. This long and varied career had exposed Pete to every facet of the motor industry, from electrical design to manufacturing operations to acquisitions and leveraged buyouts. We were extraordinarily lucky to persuade Pete to serve on our board.

The motor business we were acquiring at the time made small volumes of specialty motors, a business model at odds with its parent company's strategy of volume production. The plant was a corporate "orphan" left ignored and unmanaged for years. The deal would be a good one if we could orchestrate an operating turnaround, but that was far from certain.

When we approached Pete to consider serving on the board, he diligently went through all the information we could provide and quickly understood exactly how the business fit into the industry and what its strategic opportunities and challenges were. He advised us to pass on the investment, perceiving the significant challenges we would face in rehabilitating the business. We ignored his advice and purchased the business anyway. Pete responded that if we were dumb enough to buy an underperforming business in a concentrated, turbulent industry, the least he could do was come onto the board to try to help us fight through it.

With Pete's help, we recruited an outstanding management team and began rebuilding the business brick-by-brick. Pete has provided our team with invaluable advice on motor design, engineering processes and strategic opportunities. Most importantly, he has been a consistent voice on the board, reminding management and his fellow board members what business we are in and keeping our focus on our areas of competitive advantage.

One of the first challenges we faced as the new owners of the business was a strategic crossroads in our pool motor business. Pool and spa motors were higher volume and lower margin than the motors in our core business. In this market, we were increasingly competing against cheap motors made overseas in low wage countries and at that point we could not manufacture the motors at a competitive price domestically. Accordingly, I persuaded Pete (who already had substantial experience doing business in Asia) to join me on a trip to meet Chinese manufacturers who we believed might be able to supply us with these commodity motors at more competitive prices.

The company we had acquired was struggling and we could not afford first class airfare to Asia (a luxury Pete had become accustomed to as a global ambassador for the much larger and more successful Reliance Electric). Pete was a good sport and ended up buying an inexpensive ticket that originated in Cleveland and had stopovers in St. Louis, San Francisco, Anchorage, and Tokyo before finally landing in Shanghai. We learned from this trip that Pete "takes a lickin' and keeps on tickin'!" as the old Timex commercial used to say. He hopped off the plane and jumped right into business meeting and never missed a step.

As a China rookie, I started the trip firmly believing that partnering with a low cost manufacturing source in Asia would give us the cost basis to allow us to compete in the pool and spa business in North America. However, I noted that Pete approached our meetings with the Chinese with much more skepticism than I did. He would ask probing questions, ask to see technical data on their motors, and look into corners of their facilities they tried to omit from our tours. He was also skeptical of the spreadsheet math that seemed so compelling to me as a finance professional. He cautioned that trading with the Chinese always involved hidden costs; invariably included some element of bait-and-switch and worst of all, given the opportunity, the Chinese would take our technology and our customers.

The sourcing trip to China ultimately vindicated everything Pete had told us. The Chinese motors were of marginal quality, made with pirated designs of old western motors and, when we tried to order commercial quantities, the bait-and-switch game came into play as the Chinese increased the price. Considering these factors, as well as the need to carry high inventories and incur high shipping costs, we finally concluded that doing business with China was no bargain after all.

The cautions that Pete gave us when we pursued Chinese outsourcing still ring true today:

- The relationship with a Chinese supplier is inherently hostile, even if it is polite on the surface;
- The Chinese are not bound by normal rules of free enterprise as most enterprises are state sponsored if not state owned;
- The Chinese will commonly undermine quality by seeking to cheapen materials and taking unauthorized manufacturing shortcuts;
- Given the opportunity, the Chinese will take intellectual property and, if possible, the customers;
- Shipping costs and inventory holding costs eat up much of the supposed China labor cost saving; and
- The dramatic differences in culture, geography and time zones make it very difficult to communicate effectively to respond quickly to market changes.

This book will give the reader practical advice regarding the challenges of conducting business in China and some of the many things that should be considered - beyond the ivory-tower financial spreadsheets - when looking to outsource.

DR. PETER J. TSIVITSE

Pete Tsivitse has been a wise and thoughtful business partner to our company and when he speaks, everyone on our board listens carefully. The reader would do well to do the same when considering his advice in the pages that follow.
John M. Mueller,
Managing Partner
Partners Private Equity LLC

Preface

This book examines the following issue: does conducting business in China brings sustainable return on investment? The lure of low cost labor in China and the prospect of short term profit have caused many American businesses to transfer their manufacturing to China. However, are these gains realized long term or even in the short term? From thorough analysis and the case studies presented in the following pages, it is evident they are often not realized at all.

The contrary culture of China compared to the U.S. is well known. The disregard of human rights, poor environmental conditions, massive corruption in almost all areas (caused by their history or habit) and the present communistic military dictatorship are known. The author abhors this situation which in fact might cause the failure of present China. However, that is not the purpose of this book.

The question is simply: is conducting business with China good business or is it just poor management? The phrase an 'old China hand' refers to any Westerners with long experience in doing business with China. What I learned from an 'old China hand' is things in China are not as they appear as they are masters of deception. This warning is a reflection of the writings from the 5th century B.C., by Chinese military strategist, Sun Tzu, when he wrote: "All warfare is based on deception. Hence, when we are able to attack, we must seem unable; when using our forces, we must appear inactive; when we are near, we must make the enemy believe we are far away; when far away, we must make him believe we are near."

DR. PETER J. TSIVITSE

Sun Tzu preached that "every battle is won or lost before it's ever fought". His advice was simple: "Attack the enemy where he is unprepared and appear where you are not expected." He said it was "vital to undermine the enemy, subvert and corrupt him, sow internal discord among his leaders and destroy him without fighting him."

Many American businesses fall into this trap when making only a superficial analysis of the merits of doing business with China. It is my hope that the evidence presented in this book will aid in the avoidance of more businesses succumbing to these tricks. The consequences can be great, as often it is not only a negative return on investment, but a loss of the business itself!

Part One: Background Information

CHAPTER 1

INTRODUCTION

China presents both a large opportunity and a large problem. The Chinese can offer capabilities and resources to enhance American businesses, while solving issues in production costs and other areas. Within China are many people who will work hard and smart for long hours and low wages. There is a rapidly growing excellent technical capability, ranging from research in science to innovative design in manufacturing.

China is a work in progress and rapid progress at that! In a short period of time, they produced the largest manufacturing base in the world (obtained at the U.S. expense), the largest power plant, hydro dam, steel mill, paper mill, textile mill and the largest army. In many cases, these products of Chinese innovation are more modern than their American counterpart. They will introduce to the world, modern airplanes from regional to large jets, as well as, low cost automobiles. The total purpose of these ventures is for internal gain without compromise. Many times agreements with their American business partners are not kept, if there is a chance to benefit China internally.

The Spectrum North American (January, 2016,) states, "The C919, China's answer to the Airbus A320 and Boeing 737, is slated to have its first test flight later this year. Built by the Commercial Aircraft Corporation of China (Comac), the twin-engine airliner had its celebratory rollout last November in Shanghai. But even if this year's flight-testing goes well, don't expect to fly in a C919 right away. Indeed, if you live in Europe or the United States, don't expect to see one at your local airport".

The promise of gain to an American company using Chinese resources in these instances may not be realized and may, in fact, cause greater harm as not only the return on the investment might be negative but the American business itself may be damaged or destroyed in the process. It must always be remembered that China is a Communistic dictatorship with strong military control of the economy. Again, the 'old China hand' had warned that China's business practices are corrupt and predatory

Although, significant change is occurring and more is coming as costs are rising rapidly with increasing pressure for workers rights. This pressure can be seen not just from the U.S. but from the Chinese people as well. A middle class is developing and is demanding more of its country as China increases its affluence.

External pressure from China's customers and business partners will force China to liberalize its trade, business and human rights policies. This is not only good for China, but also for the world. However, it will decrease their competitive edge in reducing costs.

There are some additional important factors to consider:

1). China is very good at marketing itself, but often they do not deliver. (Things are not as they seem);
2). China's financial practices and goals are not the same as the U.S. Their highest priority is to create jobs to prevent civil unrest. As a result, profit is flexible in getting the order. This is not without financial merit as China has developed great cash reserves (while the U.S. has developed great debt);
3). From a base of everyone must have food to eat, a place to live, medical care and a job to an increased standard of living, China has made great gains.
4). The Chinese earn money for the common good and are patient in achieving long term goals and overcoming short term failures. This has benefitted the overall society but also leads to each individual striving for personal gain, just like the U.S.

As I gained more experience with China, I became less concerned with the culture. This came to a sudden stop when on returning from a trip through the Shanghai Passport Control, I lost control of my passport for a few minutes.

Two officers were next to each other behind a two level counter. The first officer took the passport at the top level and placed it on the lower level where it could not be seen. He examined it and transferred it to the officer next to him, who was to return it to the owner – in this case - me.

After a short time as I awaited the return of my passport, one of the officers looked up and asked me what I wanted. "My passport," I replied. To my surprise, he replied that they did not have it. Then, I noticed a Chinese man ahead of me put a green passport into his bag and then a blue passport into his bag, which I thought was strange. As he hurried away, I followed after him, grabbed his bag and pulled out the blue passport. It was my passport! The man ran away and I had no recourse other than to continue on my way to the gate.

Close call, but I learned a lesson: The official passport officers for China steal American passports! It was a lesson of corruption within agencies in China which made it difficult for me to trust them when conducting business there.

CHAPTER 2

THE PATH TO LOSS

There are three paths to conducting business with China:

1). U.S. businesses can sell American-made products to China. At first glance, this seems to be a good deal. China has a big market with little investment because the products are being made in the U.S. Yet, it is not that easy. The human cost of marketing and completing the sale in China is high. Also, the U.S. business still has to get paid enough to profit. This arrangement is often short-term as China will make the product themselves as soon as they can. This route might obtain large bookings but turning it into an actual profit is difficult.

2). U.S. businesses can make high volume of products in China to then be sold in the U.S. also known as 'outsourcing'. This outsourcing occurs because companies in China will manufacturer goods for a price that is much lower than the U.S. manufacturing. These products are often labor intensive, making China an attractive manufacturing option. However, outsourcing still requires U.S. capital and manpower to start and maintain.

3). U.S. business can enter into a joint venture and reverse engineering of American- product for sale in both the U.S. and China. This also requires U.S. capital and manpower but appears to offer a better deal as it is using Chinese capital and manpower too. However, China now owns the business. The assumption is that the U.S. will keep control of the business by keeping engineering and marketing in the U.S. Eventually, the Chinese will demand it be located in China. Soon, this will lead to double the cost and loss of business control for the U.S. Yet, all of this is overruled by the attraction of a large market that China has to offer; 1.3 billion people. However, for many products there is not one large market, but rather a collection of several markets, each one different.

Conducting business in China is very hard and costs money to overcome the difficulties. Also, China's polictical goals as a country must be considered. China is building the largest modern military in the world. The purpose of armies is to fight wars. This kind of heavy military presence in China is not to be misunderstood and contributes to the difficulty.

All of these difficulties indicate that manufacturing in China may result in costs higher than expected and the future security of the business venture debatable. Yet, the greatest threat is that China investment drains and diverts U.S. resources that can result in loss of the U.S. core business.

Former chairman and CEO of General Electric Company, Jack Welch once said, "China is obviously an enormous growth engine, but they're going to have some trouble. The country has few original brands. It's a very difficult place to do business and you can't use simple Western techniques." Mr. Welch says that companies that want to do business in China have to make a product that China wants and needs. "To go over there with a 'me too' product because it's a 'big market' is suicide".

In the following chapters, I have outlined several cases from my own experience in conducting business within Eastern Asia, particularly China. From these cases, I hope prospective business partners of China will weigh this advice carefully and use caution in any future dealing within Eastern Asia.

Part Two: Case Studies and Testimony

CHAPTER 3

CASE # 1 - THE START

In the 1980's, as a result of considerable interest in China due to their low costs and large market, the CEO/President of my company, traveled with me to China to investigate the opportunities. We started in Beijing and stayed at the Great Wall Hotel, a new, modern hotel. In the morning, we visited the Chinese ministry of metallurgy and mining with a young American who lived in China working as a guide to aid businessmen interested in China. We were welcomed and had good discussion. The opportunity for business in this area looked promising and we were told we had met 'the right people who call the shots'. We then toured the city, the Great Wall of China and Ming's Tomb and were very impressed.

After a few days touring Beijing, we traveled to Shanghai and stayed at an older, first-class hotel where they said President Reagan had also stayed. In the morning, we met with the ministry of metallurgy and mining and again had a productive meeting where they also said we were at the right place and with 'the right people who call all the shots'. This was not too different from Beijing and not unexpected.

During this time we observed the severe poverty and the inhumane treatment of the Chinese people. There were frequent executions. While this made us a little apprehensive, we still decided to proceed with the sale of our products and systems in China and to follow-up with the organization as needed. It looked like a good business deal, so we seized it.

CHAPTER 4

Case #2 - A Big Project

A few years after that initial visit, we received notice of being awarded a multimillion dollar order for the electric drive for a steel bar and rod mill to be located in Shanghai. The drive itself consisted of many components: electric motors, power electronics, controls to adjust the speed and torque and programmable, logic controller-based computers to control the entire system. The steel bars and rods were to be used for structural concrete needed for the roads and buildings which was a high priority as China was building a new infrastructure. This was going to be a big project!

In 1965, a new bar and rod mill had been built in Pittsburg, Pennsylvania. However, in 1985 it was shut down and the Chinese subsequently bought the mill (really cheap). It was a good, robust mill that could hold precise tolerances. The electric drive was to be modernized to state of the art by my company, Reliance Electric.

The Reliance system division that was to engineer and supply the drive estimated there would be no profit from this big project, leading their management to not want the order especially with so many unknowns. It would consume hours of engineering which could be used on more profitable orders. I brought this to the attention of our president who demanded we proceed forthwith. I ordered our division to proceed immediately and I would work the politics to mitigate the order.

My first step was to go to Shanghai and investigate what the Chinese would do. When I got there, I found the present mill was a 19th century structure with bare-foot workers on a dirt floor with no regard for safety! A line break could kill people.

The new mill was to be built on a site next to the old mill. At the time, this site contained tenements housing a few thousand people who were to be removed. Upon returning to Cleveland, I informed the system people that despite my efforts I could not get the order cancelled but it would take years to build the new plant. I advised them to keep working on the project to schedule. However, less than a year later, we were advised the site had been cleared and construction on the new plant was ready to begin.

I returned to Shanghai and discussed with the mill people their plans to build, operate and service the new, high-tech mill. They had neither a plan to service the mill nor the people to do so. At that point, I reported to my company president and recommended that we cancel the order as the project would fail for lack of service and our reputation would suffer. He told me to go to Tokyo and meet with the chairman of our joint venture company in Japan who was considered a world-famous scientist. The Tokyo chairman was the founder of a post-World War II company that supplied high tech vacuum equipment for various applications ranging from a furnace brazing to semiconductor manufacturing. After his review, the Tokyo chairman advised that I return to Shanghai and see the head of a local school of engineering, Fudan University

I followed his advice and went back to Shanghai to meet with head of the college who agreed to supply ongoing service to the mill using his pool of engineering graduate students. It was decided the students would start as soon as the construction began as this would offer valuable training for them. This was the start of a new joint venture company in China for the big project. At this point, we had no choice but to go ahead full speed.

Then the problems began. The first issue was the repair of several large DC motors powering the mill. They had been brought to China on the deck of the ship that took them across the Pacific and were soaked with salt water from the trip. These were the original 1965 motors made by General Electric and were not Reliance Electric's responsibility. Yet, we were the company on the job site and therefore the Chinese demanded we repair the motors. After several days lost in debate over this, we agreed to repair the motors in order to avoid a penalty on the project schedule. The second issue was a matter of locations. We planned to do the work at a Hong Kong repair shop but the Chinese demanded we do the repairs in Shanghai. Again, we were forced to agree. This is one of many examples illustrating the predatory and corrupt nature of Chinese business.

Approximately one year later, the project was complete and it was the most modern, largest and fastest bar and rod mill in the world. All of this was done with 1965 Pittsburgh iron and a state of the art controller developed in Cleveland, Ohio. We were paid only a portion of what we charged but the project was finished.

Several years later, we received a duplicate order for a second mill. The Chinese requested we travel to Shanghai to sign the order. The company president and I did so and were proud to tour the mill which was outstanding and we enjoyed much praise from the Chinese. This was followed by a friendly discussion in the tea room and more positive feedback about our past work.

After we had been talking in the tea room for some time, I asked our Hong Kong sales person about signing the order for the second mill project. Through a period of translation, we were told there was a small change of plans. We were to supply the latest controller. I asked if there was anything wrong with the present controller. They responded "No, but we want the latest and the best". I explained our new controller was still in the lab and had just finished alpha testing so it was still awaiting beta testing in the field. We had tried to have this testing done at American steel mills from Cleveland to Pittsburg to Chicago and Baltimore but had not received acceptance. The opportunity to beta test a new controller was turned down by these American companies because the belief was the old controller was good enough and there was no need for the cost and risk of a new controller.

The Chinese management in that room already knew of our lack of acceptance for beta testing our new controller in America. Subsequently, they offered to be the beta test site as part of the new order. I was not comfortable with the idea of beta testing a high tech product thousands of miles from home. However, as this was the demand for the new order, I had to agree. We then jointly signed the order including their testing of the new controller.

My head was low as I left the tea room and a young Chinese engineer at the mill that I had gotten to know well put his arm around my shoulder. He said, "Peter, my friend, you have just received a very large order and yet you do not look happy. Did we do something wrong?" I explained, "No, you did well. But, I am discouraged that no U.S. steel mill which has even greater need of the new controller and the technology and money it would provide, would not take our offer for a beta test. Why would China do so and the U.S. would not?" The young Chinese engineer answered, "We have faith in the future and they do not. So, we are willing to make the investment and take the risk."

As a result, China is now a world leader in steel production and the U.S. is not. I concluded that the problem in this case is not China, not the U.S. government, not American labor or American technology. It was the management of U.S. business who were not willing to make the investment, take the risk and work hard to advance the business of making steel. It was poor U.S. management!

CHAPTER 5

CASE # 3 - ELECTRIC MOTOR OUTSOURCING

In the mid 1980's, we were ready to build the last new plant of a five year modernization project. The project had gone well with four new plants on line. The last plant was an important part of our product line, composed of three segments: *standard, modified from standard* and *custom*. We sold *standard* at our price because the motor supply in this segment was greater than demand; we were the market leader in *modified*; we picked our *custom* carefully as the engineering and risk were high.

The plant to be built was a replacement of a forty year old volume plant that produced the low end (in size) of the *custom* segment with a fair amount of the *standard* segment which were the most common in the industry. This new plant was to be designed with state of the art equipment and systems to produce *modified* product in a short cycle. This would help maintain our leadership in this segment. However, the *standard* product volume was quite high in the industry and the price very low. The sales people advocated we use the new plant to compete in this area. They were paid on volume, not profit.

Throughout our history, management and marketing had structured the business to focus on the *modified* segment and developed a premium, highly profitable company which conflicted with the sales goal at times. Sales, marketing, engineering and manufacturing were organized to excel in this area. This required delivery time that was competitive to the *non-modified*, great flexibility with highest quality and performance while also being rewarded with high income. At times, management lost focus and took too much *standard* segment business which lowered profits and shortened the tenure of management.

As the new plant was being approved, the sales team pushed for the *standard* segment option. They were good at selling and they obtained the attention of upper management. This executive team was new to the business and did not fully understand or appreciate the business model. They also obtained the support of some of the engineering and manufacturing people, particularly those we had hired from large companies such as General Electric and General Motors. However, we were not in that class size. The *modified* segment of business required being on the top of that business all the time and it was very demanding. The result was we were requested to design the plant for *standard* segment products. This was a bad decision and we resisted but it was not enough.

To circumvent this order, we aggressively pursued outsourcing to other areas of the world ranging from other parts of Eastern Asia, to south of the U.S. border to Europe. We examined several companies, before finally settling on a company in Taiwan which had engineering and manufacturing technology obtained from retired consultants from our company, Reliance Electric. Those were men we knew and appreciated. That company made an offer we could not refuse. Their price was equal to our material costs even though their material was better than ours.

We obtained reluctant approval from sales and management to outsource this motor as our *non-modified* offering. We were then free to build the *modified* motor plant in the U.S. (which met expectations) and develop a *standard* segment business with the Taiwanese company to import their product. This required a large team for the U.S. plant and also a team for the Taiwan plant. We did both, but it slowed work in the U.S. plant.

Work started on the Taiwan motor project with minor changes in cosmetics such as paint color and some sheet metal contours. The basic motor design had been produced for years and required no change. The logistic system and marketing were established and market introduction commenced. In a little more than a year, we were up and running. We worked through early quality and delivery problems and two years after initial contact, we were at rated production for about ten years.

After a few years, our supplier requested a significant price increase claiming increase in material costs. Since material was a world commodity which was not increasing at the time, we knew there was some other reason. Under our protest, they admitted they had priced too low. We had no choice but to accept the increased material costs.

Several years later, they requested another price increase, this time due to labor. We accepted this increase in costs with the promise by the supplier they would work on finding a way to decrease the labor cost. They responded by moving production to mainland China where they had many issues with quality control. After a few more years, the supplier requested another price increase, this time it was due to inflation.

During this same time period, our U.S. plants were reducing costs, until the price from Taiwan/China was now greater than our costs in the U.S. Subsequently, we moved productions back to the U.S. and the relationship with Taiwan/China came to an end.

It was a short slide for a long climb. Overall, we broke even but it had left long-term damage to our business. We had diluted our premium position as a reliable supplier of quality products because we had engaged in marketing a commodity product. There was also a reaction from the commodity product competitors as they started to invade our premium product area. Although the competitors had a lower valued product and service, it still took away some of our business. The greatest loss was the manpower spent on outsourcing that should have been spent on improvement of our U.S. product. The people required for the failed project were our best- the hardest working and most innovative. All in all, the project was a mistake. On the surface, it appeared to be a break-even scenario but in reality, the project was a loss because of the harm it did to our business.

Who was at fault? Officially, it was the Taiwanese who did not meet their commitments. Yet, we knew they would be devious with pricing. We were aware of their strategy to price low to establish a relationship and then manipulate the prices after the deal was made. It may seem our executive management was at fault because they ordered the plant mission change. However, that is what they do. The real fault was my own. I knew this motor outsourcing was a bad idea but I did not convince the organization to avoid this problem. I should have tried harder even to the point of losing my position. But I liked my position and my ego forced me to go with the clever option, Asia.

It was poor management on my part.

CHAPTER 6

Case #4 - Small Motor Manufacture

In 2005, an opportunity arose for an independent small motor company located in the Midwest to expand their market by manufacturing in China. The small motors were 1/4 to 5 HP. single and PolyPhase AC induction. The business focused on *modified* motors to customer requirement. They were moving away from higher volume *standard* motors to improve margins with more premium and less commodity. The manufacturing plant, as well as headquarters, was in an old unionized plant based on World War II technology. In spite of this, it was well managed and did a good job with excellent quality and delivery while maintaining competitive performance at enhanced prices. However, the market was limited which restricted growth to inflation and share gain.

At that time, the housing market in the Sun-Belt was booming. The sales department of this small motor company realized an opportunity for swimming pool motors. These motors are on the low end of the commodity market where prices were too low for the company to make a profit. Pool motors were being made in China and several Chinese companies approached the small motor company to make the motors for them to sell to the U.S. market. Although this kind of business was not in this company's focus, the Chinese prices were so low that it appeared to be a good opportunity. A team was formed to go to China and investigate. I was asked to be on the team and so, onward again to China.

Our team was well-received in China. We were wined and dined and offered anything we desired. (I told them I was too old and tired.) The next morning, we toured the facility which was a work in progress. It was large and impressive with modern machinery. We estimated it was a one billion dollar project to serve both the Chinese and western market. The money was from the Chinese government. We were very impressed.

However, most of the product was made from parts manufactured in the old, original plant about one hundred miles north. We asked to see this plant but were refused. We persisted until finally we were taken to the original plant. What we saw when we arrived felt like a place out of the Dark Ages. There were young men and women working in very unsafe, slave-like conditions. In the casting foundry, they carried molten iron by hand-held ladles. In the stamping plant, they had no safety controls on the presses. That was an anatomy for losing hands and feet. Yet, that was the source for much of the new plant product.

The Chinese offered to produce a product at a price less than our material costs. So, we agreed to test and evaluate seventeen of their motors. The motors arrived in the U.S. late and required reworking to be tested. After some time, they were judged satisfactory for a pool motor. At that point, we sent a purchasing and marketing team with a large order to China. The team returned empty-handed because the Chinese had doubled the price. Again, a short slide for a long climb but we had relearned the lesson of Chinese business.

CHAPTER 7

Case #5 - An Opportunity

Early in our Leverage Buyout Phase, Westinghouse Electric Company offered the sale of their electric motor business. The general manager of our motor division brought this opportunity to me but I rejected the offer. He persisted and eventually convinced me to visit each of the three Westinghouse motor plants. There was a small motor plant in Lima, Ohio, a medium-sized motor plant in Buffalo, New York and a large motor plant in Austin, Texas. We traveled to and toured each plant but I was still not interested. The medium-sized motor plant in Buffalo appeared to offer some good business but it was in great disarray in its functions including sales, engineering, product and the plant itself. Apparently, the plant had problems with their northern union, so they had moved the winding to Mexico. This change caused confusion and problems, which had the Buffalo plant blaming the Mexico division and the Mexico plant blaming the Buffalo division. I wanted no part of that. However, Westinghouse persisted and offered their medium-sized motors at a very low price. We ended up purchasing their customer list but not the plant, product, or people. The deal maker was Westinghouse's commitment to sell only our motor through Wesco, their distribution house of five years.

One year later, I reported to the Board of Directors at Reliance Electric that we had obtained a 25% increase in medium-sized motor sales which made us the market leader. We had paid off the acquisition in one year, making excellent return. We had worked the opportunity and had made a great gain! The board responded with praise and asked

"What motor company can we buy next?" I answered "None." My response was not well received. Rather, the board directed me to purchase the General Electric Motor business. Immediately, I scheduled a trip to Fort Wayne, Indiana to call on the president of GE Motors.

CHAPTER 8

CASE #6 - GENERAL ELECTRIC KOREA

As requested by the Board of Directors, I traveled to Fort Wayne to meet with the president and the development manager of the General Electric Motors. Upon entering his office, the president indicated that he did not know why I had come. He reported that GE had studied our company and had decided not to buy it. I responded with, "I am not here to sell our motor business. I am here to buy yours." He was shocked and stated that GE would never sell its motor business. He went even futher telling me that he had the commitment and funds to make GE Motors the leading motor company in the U.S. I persisted and said "You should save your money as your plan will not work. The GE motor business is old and cold and cannot be fixed." At that point, the development manager said that he was interested in what I had to say. I continued in a good discussion about the reasons I thought GE should sell their motor business, emphasizing our focus on median AC motors. As my arguments gained traction, they reacted with the claim they had a new innovative design to increase motor performance and lower costs. Therefore, they would be able to compete with any other motor company.

Recently, GE had developed a new motor with unique design, had high performance and low estimated costs. It was to be made in South Korea in a joint venture with a South Korean company. They showed me an exceptional motor with clever engineering. Yet, I could see it would be difficult to produce, with high costs. The GE manager's explanation was that South Korea was going to solve the high cost issue. I argued I did not think their arrangement would work and they countered by inviting me to travel to Korea with their marketing manager to determine if my concerns were valid.

The trip to the plant resulted in a good review of the production process and the physical plant itself. However, of greater importance was the Korean engineers' statement that the motor design was difficult but they could make it at extra cost. This response was reported to the GE management team and who showed concern about the higher cost for production. Nevertheless, they decided to continue with the Korean joint venture. This concluded our talks with General Electric to buy their motor business.

Sometime later, the GE/Korean motor business joint venture came apart. General Electric exited the motor business and Korea kept the work. In the meantime, GE had shut down its U.S. motor plant and now had to find a new source of supply. The end result of their venture with Asian manufacturing was that GE spent a lot of money with no product to show and lost their U.S. position in the motor business.

I concluded the overall design of the GE motor had merit but needed further joint design and considerable manufacturing development by the U.S. engineers working with the Korean plant personnel. Unfortunately, a joint venture with Asian manufacturing made this very difficult.

If General Electric had made the same investments in their U.S. plants and products, they might have regained their leadership in the motor business. But as a result of making the investment in Asia, they lost their leadership and a key part of their motor business.

CHAPTER 9

CASE # 7 - CHINA SURVEY

In 1980, Reliance Electric Company was purchased by Exxon. Approximately five years later, a Reliance management team purchased the company back from Exxon and then went into a successful Leverage Buyout followed by an Initial Public Offering. After that, they began to operate as a public company with stock on the New York Exchange. All of this was positive for the company and shareholders.

In the early 1990's, there were some internal problems coupled with a soft market and the stock price could not meet expectations. Growth was low even though customers continued to value Reliance Electric products. An expert in international business from a leading university was contracted to help with growth. His recommendation was to do business in China. At the time, we were using China for selected large systems orders at our price. The expert's recommendation was to make an investment in China on a broader scale.

A team was organized to travel to China to examine the opportunities. This team contained key people from each division and I was fortunate to be chosen to lead this team. We traveled to several parts of China and examined several businesses. We could not find many U.S. companies making a good profit, even after years of investment and some even at the expense of their main business.

An example of this is in the Chinese cell phone business. At the time of our visit, a leading cell phone supplier in the U.S. and had, made a very large investment in China in return for the promise of exclusive rights to the market. My team met with American cell phone supplier in their new, modern building near Beijing. We had several detailed reviews of their business. The outcome was they had the very large Chinese cell phone market but could not make a profit on it in China. However, the American cell phone supplier reported that the cell phone chip was made in the U.S. and that this product was profitable. Our concern was that the Chinese would soon decide to have the chips made in China as well. The American cell phone supplier countered, saying that would never happen because they had a contract in place for just that reason.

A few years later, we learned that this leading American cell phone supplier was making a multi-million dollar investment into cell phone chip manufacture in China. I asked our contact with the American cell phone supplier about the terms of their contract with China to only manufacture the chip in America. He informed me the Chinese had told them, "Your contract, not ours" resulting in the American company losing the profit of U.S. chip production to China. After all the investments in time, manpower, and money, American cell phone company would also eventually lose the exclusive rights to the Chinese cell phone market. This ultimately led to their downfall and they were no longer one of the leading cell phone companies in the U.S. The Chinese venture had distracted leading American cell phone company from their focus and they lost their core competitive edge. This also weakened their efforts on the digital cell phone development.

The team investigating expanding the business in China had recommended significant investments not be made. Instead they suggested a continuous watch be put in place and we would continue to take orders at our price when available. The executive board accepted our recommendation and this became the company policy. We returned to working on our internal problems to make progress. As our results improved, expectations were raised and some individuals challenged this company policy. The consequences of this are shown in the following case.

CHAPTER 10

CASE #8 - THE COMMUNICATIONS VENTURE

One of Reliance's fastest growing groups was communications group. It consisted of three businesses: the battery charger, the connecter/suppressor and the multiplexing digital division.

There was a bright, well-educated, energetic young man working at the corporate staff level. In order to gain experience and further his career, he was put in charge of communications operations. He started his role by making several significant changes. Some of these were good changes and others were not so good, but none of them were detrimental.

After some time in the operations department, he proposed a plan to the management group to set up business in China. He presented a strong plan including three joint ventures, one for each division of communications. This was in conflict with our China policy established following the events of the American cell phone supplier. Yet, this up-and-coming manager was well-liked and after several rejections he obtained approval for his plan.

After great effort at the expense of communications operations in the U.S., the plan was executed with three joint ventures in China. Unfortunately, the promised results never came.

More than a reasonable time passed, the operations manager was removed from the China work and the communications group started to withdraw from China. This departure was more difficult than expected and a veteran communications engineer, with management experience and an international background, was put in charge of the China retreat. I spoke with the engineer after the exodus from China and he explained the initial joint ventures were well-planned and implemented. However, communications was bound to fail because the Chinese do not want joint ventures in their country. China wants to own the business themselves.

The communications venture cost the company time and money as it took valuable resources away from the U.S.-based business. All along, the Chinese were being educated by the U.S. communications group.

DR. PETER J. TSIVITSE

Dr. Peter J. Tsivitse at the SuperConductivity Lab in Shanghi, China.

Dr. Peter J. Tsivitse at the JC Design Lab, Fudan University in Shanghi, China

CONDUCTING BUSINESS WITH CHINA

Class at Fudan University in Shanghi, China with Dr. Tsivitse in the front middle.

Dr. Tsivitse meeting with President Hug at Fudan University (1990)

Dr. Peter Tsivitse standing behind the Ministry of Metals in Beijing, China

Driving through the streets of Beijing, China (1990)

CONDUCTING BUSINESS WITH CHINA

Dr. Peter Tsivitse meeting with Yieh Phui in Beijing, China

The Great Wall of China section in Beijing, China

CHAPTER 11

CASE #9 - THE POOL MOTOR

In 2001, my wife and I had a swimming pool built for our home in Florida. It is a very good lap pool with a full complement of filter, pump and water fall, which are driven by a 1.5 HP AC motor. The initial pool motor was built in Tipp City, Ohio by a company called A.O. Smith Corporation. It lasted eight years before it failed which was seven years more than the one year warranty.

The replacement motor was also from A.O. Smith Corporation but it was built in Mexico. This Mexican-made motor lasted three years. The second replacement was another A.O. Smith motor but it was made in China. This China-made motor worked for fourteen months, two months longer than its warranty. At that time, I had to pay approximately five hundred dollars for the third motor. This new motor was another A.O. Smith motor made in China. In addition to the quality problems I experienced with the last China-made pool motor, this replacement came with a new problem. After the motor ran for a short time, it would trip the thermal switch. The motor was overheating due to the current draw being 25% over the nameplate rating, which led to premature overheating and failure. None of the other pool motors had done this.

After some investigation, I realized this China-made motor was built in a period of time when material costs rose exceptionally high. It appears the Chinese reduced the material quality to save costs. This then caused the current to become high which caused the overheating. The motor did not meet the specifications and should not have been put on the market. The Chinese had cheated.

My last replacement was a pool motor made in the U.S. which works well. The time, money and frustration I experienced were not worth the savings of a motor built in China. It would have been more economical for me if I had been able to replace the initial pool motor with another A.O. Smith Corp. motor made in the U.S., even if the cost of the motor is greater than a China-made version. My service bill for the problems associated with the motors made in China has resulted in choosing a U.S. company for my replacement pool motor. I do not think that A.O. Smith Corporation has profited by making their motors in China.

CHAPTER 12

CASE #10 - AMERICAN SUPERCONDUCTOR COMPANY (AMSC)

The story of American Superconductor Company (AMSC) doing business with China is one with some tragedy. In order to understand the events of this case, a little background information on the concept of superconductivity is necessary. Superconductors are materials with very little resistance to electric current flow when cooled cryogenically. Reducing electric energy loss and permitting smaller, more efficient products. With the world's demand for energy and material, superconductors become quite valuable.

Over one hundred years ago, a Dutch Physicist, Dr. Onnes, discovered superconductivity in mercury loses resistance when cooled to 4 degrees on the Kelvin scale (or -452 F) just a scant 4 degrees above absolute zero. In the mid-20th century, certain combinations of Niobium and Titanium (NbTi) were found to become superconductive at approximately 20 K. Westinghouse Electric Company developed a wire of NbTi used in a high-energy particle accelerator. However, the costs of cryogenic cooling were so expensive this type of superconductor was limited to laboratory and medical use. In 1986, an IBM laboratory developed a ceramic copper-oxide compound that became superconductive at 30 K. This reduced the cooling considerably, increasing the economic viability, and ease of commercialization, of superconductors.

In Boston, MIT joined the development of high temperature superconductivity (HTSC) and a researcher in material science developed a ceramic-based, silver-coated unique HTSC wire. Although he was a professor, he left MIT to start a company that would go on to commercialize the HTSC wire. This company would focus on low loss power cable and high efficiency motors.

They obtained startup money from a venture capitalist and the U.S. government. Excellent progress was made with increasing the capability of the wire and a new plant was built for its manufacture. They made several power cable installations with power companies and developed AC motors to 5,000 HP with a fraction of the loss compared to copper-wire based cables and motors. However, they could not develop an industrial motor business because the motor users did not value the low loss motors. Although the economics showed a good payback from original price to energy cost, they did not want to make the investment.

The American Superconductor Company then decided to pursue the military market where the U.S. Navy would value the energy and lower weight of the motor. With the lower loss, the HTSC motors required less material and them smaller and lighter than their competition. The AMSC was rewarded a significant contract from the U.S. Navy to provide the electrical power system for ship propulsion including motors, control and power electronics. They successfully made a 50,000 HP drive which passed the Navy tests. Unfortunately, the demands of the Mid-East wars halted further work.

Following this setback, the AMSC purchased a company with power electronic system capability, as the power transmission business became increasingly active. In addition, the American superconductor company purchased a wind mill company which added to their business.

> "American Superconductor Corporation (AMSC) is a provider of mega-watt scale solutions that lower the cost of wind power and enhance the performance of the power grid. It operates in two business units: Wind and Grid. Wind business segment enables manufacturers to field wind turbines with power output, reliability and affordability. Grid business segment enables electric utilities and renewable energy project developers to connect, transmit and distribute power with efficiency, reliability and affordability. The Company's wind and power grid products and

services provide reliability, security, efficiency and affordability to its customers. The Company manufactures products using two core technologies: Power Module programmable power electronic converters and its Amperium HTS (High Temperature Superconductor) wires." (New York Times, 12/14/07)

However, the American Superconductor Company was not satisfied with their sales and financial results. Impressed by the China hype, they contracted a consultant to facilitate doing business in China and proceeded to make a major effort there. The initial results in China were good. The sales increased and with high sales came high profits. But, when the Chinese would not pay per the contract the profits became losses. The American superconductor company's stock severely decreased. They then started litigation with a major Chinese company, Sinovel Wind Group. This lawsuit moved through the complex Chinese courts. In the process, Sinovel Wind Group was charged with stealing trade secrets from the American company. As of mid-2013, the litigation continued. In January 2016, this American superconductor company was featured on CBS "60 Minutes" as an example of systematic theft by the Chinese military.

This was such a major setback for this U.S. company which had been making good progress before the drive for higher financial results took over. They were the leaders in the field of HTSC with power applications in place. They were on the right path but they got off track. Notably, they were ahead of the national recognition of the value for energy-saving products such as there. But, that time has come now. The windmill business of the American Superconductor Company is now a limited contribution whereas reduction of power transmission and use is much broader and far reaching. TheAMSC could have been a highly valuable contributor to the national effort to save on energy if they had been patient and not been distracted by the hype to do business in China.

CHAPTER 13

CASE #11 - THE ELECTRIC LAWN MOWER

In early 2000, a leading U.S. manufacturer of lawn mowers and tractors using gasoline engines began development of an electric battery driven motor lawn mower in order to protect against government regulations on gas engine emissions. As electric batteries are as much as 70 times heavier than gasoline providing the same energy, weight needed to be taken out of the rest of lawn mower to make a viable mower.

The development team purchased a European design for a lightweight commutator DC electric motor. The company had excellent mechanical capability to make gasoline engines but they were deficient in their understanding of electric motors. This lack of knowledge led them to purchase a design that did not adhere to the principles of good electric motor design. Electric motors make torque at speed to produce horsepower. The torque is the product of magnetic flux and current in the conductors. The magnetic path carrying flux is normally made of electric grade steel which has several thousand times the flux ability of air. The European design did not use electrical steel in order to reduce weight. But, this also reduced the flux which required many more conductor turns. This caused dangerous electric sparking at the commutator. The design was novel with a clever but complicated winding.

I was hired as a Consultant to assist in finding a solution for the electric sparking and in time a modified design was generated to solve the problem. However, the design was complicated and held high costs to manufacture. The company decided to make the motor in China in order to cut down on the labor cost. After almost two years of working with China on the manufacture, they finally received a satisfactory motor the company was willing to produce. At this point, the development of the China business had taken the time and efforts of their best electric engineer through many trips to China. This meant that he was not available for work needed at the U.S.-based business.

Finally, the company gave China the orders for production and the Chinese responded with the claim that the U.S. company was in default of the contract due to the late startup of production. The claim had merit but the Chinese were also at fault and partially responsible for the delay. Nonetheless, the business was lost to the Chinese. They would not negotiate with the U.S. company and China now owns the business. It was a short slide for a long haul or maybe no slide at all. The lack of knowledge regarding electric motors combined with doing business with China led to their failure. The company had tried to take an easy way out of a high cost design by manufacturing in China and it did not work.

CHAPTER 14

CASE #12 - THE ELECTRIC CAR

At an early age, I was attracted to electricity and automobiles. My heroes were Thomas Edison and Henry Ford. I was always reading and experimenting with electricity. For example, I powered an incandescent lamp bulb with no vacuum and blew all the fuses in my parent's house. I did not know why that happened.

Logic followed that as a teenager, I dreamed of a car powered by electricity. I knew about the battery powered car made by Baker Electric Company in Cleveland, Ohio but, I was ignorant of the science between batteries and gasoline. I did not know that gasoline has about 70 times the energy density of batteries. So, I kept dreaming of an electric car.

In the early 20th century, the advent of low cost oil prompted the Ford Company to develop a low-cost, reliable, easy to drive Model T car using an internal combustion engine fueled by gasoline. This was the basis for cars for a hundred years and the electric battery powered motor was relegated to golf carts.

In my early years as an electric motor designer, I became an expert in underground, coal mine, electric traction motors. Electricity was the main power for the motor because gasoline was too explosive for coal mines. I continued on with the electric traction motor but not for cars because that was not my company's business.

When Exxon acquired Reliance Electric in 1980, they gave us their electric car development work which then became my responsibility. We made prototype electric traction drives for GM, Ford, Chrysler and Toyota. It went well but Exxon stopped the project when oil dropped to

$10.00 per barrel. So, I stayed in non-automotive motors until I retired in 1995.

After I retired from Reliance, I became a consultant and worked for a variety of other companies. Some involved in electric traction for mainly non-automotive applications. Then, in 2009 a friend called me with an exciting opportunity for an application of electric motors. I went to Detroit to meet with him and he told me his company had received a contract to build electric traction drivers for cars in the Midwest. The motors and their prototypes had been developed in China and given approval by their U.S. customer. The job was to "make the motors to print" in the U.S.

I was directed to find a source of supply in the Midwest leading me to visit several U.S. motor companies with no success. The companies would not take on the work because they claimed it "wasn't their kind of business". Therefore I recommended we make a facility to build the electric motor. I presented a plan for a state of the art plant to meet the requirement of automotive costs and quality. This was approved by management and I was to work for approximately three years to produce the plant.

The company then commenced the work of design and building the plant with me and a colleague working with them. The work progressed well but after forty years of motor work, I knew the design must be right for the plant to succeed. I focused on the design by examining design details, tests results and the prototype motors we were sporadically receiving from China.

We found the electric motor design by the Chinese to be full of errors. The prototypes made in China were not made to print. There had been changes made to the design in China the U.S. had not sanctioned. The motor prototypes ran hot during tests. And most importantly, the design was unnecessarily difficult to manufacture.

In response to these problematic issues, we presented a plan to correct the errors beginning with locating engineering in the U.S. plant. There was a surplus of mechanical engineers in Detroit and that part of the team came together well. Electric motor designers however could not be found. The solution was to bring the original electric engineer from China to join our team in the U.S. This appeared to be a simple solution on the surface, but we soon discovered this Chinese engineer stopped all the design changes needed to make the motor manufacturable. It was his original design and he would not agree to modifications.

Issues with the Chinese engineer resulted in the hire of a young electrical engineer, also from Asia, who was able to assist in developing design changes to improve the costly unreliable design. We then presented the plan to improve the original design. The main items in the plan were not approved by the company because the customer needed to approve the changes as well. The company did not want to irritate the customer with the design changes so the manufacture proceeded without the main changes. As predicted, the production was over cost and the product had reliability issues.

During field road tests, the customer complained the motor losses were much higher than expected. The application was an urban car, for city or town driving at speeds from 0 to 45 mph. However, the motor was designed to also operate above 45 mph, to double that speed at maximum power.

The motor type selected was a brushless DC motor well suited to above the base speed (45 mph) and is used in hybrid cars for that duty. The brushless DC motor has high losses at 0 to 45 mph which is the purpose of the urban car. This motor uses neodymium iron permanent magnets. China is the world supplier for this material. It is very expensive and is the highest material cost in the motor. To compound this problem, China put an export duty on this material which made it the key high cost factor in the motor (more than copper and electrical steel). The brushless DC motor not only had high losses at low speeds but high costs. It was simply the wrong motor for the job!

As China was the only significant producer of rare earth materials, they held the rest of the world hostage. How did the U.S., formerly the leader of development of this material get in this position? The first neodymium magnets Reliance used in high-power density motors were produced in the U.S. It was expensive and its use was therefore limited. The producers found the cost was high, and with a limited market, they did what most U.S. businesses would do. They stopped producing the material even though the potential looked good. So was the cost of the early microprocessor high but people with vision and government support continued to where it is the basis of our present information systems and devices. The payback was also quite nice. On the other hand, China saw the potential and with government support, made it the national effort to develop the technology and production to become the worlds predominate supplier of rare earth materials. They own the market and can now charge what they want and they do.

Today, not only do electric cars depend on rare earth magnets to produce high power and lighter motors, but many of our defense systems depend on it for its power density needed by our missiles, high performance fighter planes, and computer systems. The U.S. defense depends on materials made in China! China can not only charge what they want but can limit the supply as they want which on occasion they do and there is nothing we can do about it!.

Yes, China is predatory but they paid the price to obtain that position. They invested in the future. The U.S. also saw the potential but would not invest and ultimately missed a great opportunity. That's poor management!

An A.C. induction motor was proposed as it has lower losses for the urban car duty and uses commonly available materials. Therefore, it was much lower in costs. We designed such a motor and proposed it to management. It was again rejected out of fear these changes might irritate the customer. The electric car with the original design from China is in production with very low sales due to high price and a lower range due to high losses. It appears that the fault belongs to the wrong motor design originally done by the Chinese. The production orientation and demands made correcting the design in the U.S. were too difficult. The real fault is with the U.S. management who chose to do business with China in the first place.

CHAPTER 15

CASE #13 THE GERMAN WAY

As a teenager during WW2, I was impressed with the might of Germany even as I prayed for their defeat. During my time in the U.S. Army after WW2, I never went to Europe as I served in the Pacific side. My first opportunity to see Germany came in 1977 as the new manager of the Toledo Scale group of Reliance Electric Company. I was charged with fixing a broken business. We worked very hard and in time saw some improvement but not enough to make corporate happy.

I was responsible for the European operation of Toledo Scale which included Germany and I visited and worked there frequently. On one of my visits to the German plant located in Cologne, I was asked to have lunch with Mrs. Primm, the wife of the deceased founder of Toledo Work. The U.S. Toledo Scale Company had purchased Toledo Work but Mrs. Primm still owned 49% of Toledo Work.

I had a delightful lunch with Mrs. Primm at her house which was similar to the home of my mother, an immigrant from Europe and a pre WW2 U.S. citizen. Toward the end of the lunch, Mrs. Primm said "You are doing very well with record profits but are making a mistake." I replied that making profits was my job and that she was receiving record dividend. Mrs. Primm argued that she did not want more dividends but rather we should invest more into the business to insure the future of the company. "That is the German way", she said.

I accepted her point and invested more into the Toledo Work sales, marketing, engineering, product and plant. I also increased investment to the U.S. business. In a reasonable time we obtained a good return both in the U.S. and in Europe. This came at the expense of much pressure from Reliance Electric executive management that questioned my actions. However, my direct management, the corporate executive V.P., a very wise and good boss supported me. I was then promoted to Corporate Vice President. The investment in Toledo Work paid off as the business became healthy and a contributor to Reliance Electric's total results.

As I ponder the "German way" of investing in future versus the "U.S. way" of short term maximum return (even at the risk of future results), I am reminded of the past. Consider that Germany at half the U.S. size is the leader of the larger European economy. While the U.S. debt is at record levels, Germany supports the weaker European nations. While the U.S. economy depends on consumer spending, Germany created wealth by large exports. All this with a large social program and wages equal or greater than the U.S.

Many would say that this is the result of a very industrious work ethic, a conservative approach and high discipline. These factors certainly contribute but I believe the real contribution is Mrs. Primm's "German way", to invest wisely in the future.

Americans buy German products at high prices, such as German cars: BMW, Audi, and Mercedes Benz. Other products such as medical equipment are also purchased by the U.S. Recently, I needed an MRI examination and a medical doctor recommended making sure the MRI equipment is at least 1 Tesla because a high flux density level is needed to get a detailed picture. To my delight and surprise, it was a 3 Tesla which has both a high flux density level and high resolution. It was made by the German Company, Seimens.

At the time I started working in the electric power industry, the leaders were Westinghouse Electric, Allis Chamlers and General Electric. It was my professional goal to work for one of these companies but my mentor recommended that I work for a smaller company such as Reliance Electric and Engineering Company because it had more opportunity. His advice was invaluable.

At this time, only General Electric has survived in the U.S. industry and the world leader is German corporation, Seimens. From the ashes of WW2, Germany has become a world leader in the electric power industry. Meanwhile, the United States, once the leader during WW2, has slipped badly. This leads me to believe we should try the 'German way' and reinvest in the future of the U.S. instead of investing in other countries such as China.

This would be good management and good business!

CHAPTER 16

CASE #14 THE ELECTRIC TRUCK

Electric truck is the common name of large vehicles used mainly in open pit coal copper and other ore mines. They use diesel powered electric wheel motors much like the power system used in railroad systems. Except, they are an order of magnitude in power rating, smaller and run on huge, rubber tires. About a 50 years ago, they were initially developed for 75- ton vehicles, as this power exceeded the ability of mechanical drives. They have the flexibility to go into a mine unloaded, load up and power out with a large amount adapting to the changes in mine contour that rail vehicles could not.

To meet the ever growing need for bigger trucks to haul larger loads more economically, they have grown to 500 tons, which is the weight of ore they can carry. Add to that, the weight of an unloaded truck which is about equal in weight to the total weight of a loaded truck could be 1000 tons (one Kilo ton). (They really should be called diesel electric trucks and should not be confused with battery driven electric cars which are much smaller.) These trucks were initially made in the western U.S. as that's where the mines were. Now, they are used worldwide.

The electric power system was developed by the U.S. companies. The company's engineering, manufacturing and application was mainly done by western miners and it was outstanding. They did the job, were economical and wanted by the world market. Not all innovation was in Silicon Valley, although modern computers are used in the truck control system. This was hands on work using the best of modern technology. This was a representation of old American spirit of progress.

At that time, there were two companies in Euclid, Ohio (a suburb of Cleveland); White Motor Company and Reliance Electric Company. White Motor Company was a manufacturer of off-highway equipment including large off-highway trucks but not electric trucks. Reliance Electric Company was a manufacturer of electric motor drives but again not for large electric trucks. Both companies were very aggressive with excellent, progressive management who wanted to grow their business.

At a meeting between their top executives, White Motor Company proposed the joint development of a large electric truck. They saw the need for a truck larger than the 100-ton which was the largest in use at that time. Reliance Electric Company was in the mining business and also agreed that the mines had an insatiable appetite for larger machinery.

The 100-ton truck used the largest, lightest diesel engine available. White Motors proposed the use of a 2000 kw turbine but it ran at 13,000 to 21, 000 RPM. This was much faster than the 2,000 RPM diesel engine, so it could not use generators with wound coil rotating armatures. Reliance proposed an unconventional type of generator of the inductor alternator type which did not have rotating coils but instead used a solid iron rotor.

The project was agreed upon, teams formed, and work commenced. It was finished on time and within budget. The 200-ton electric trucks were delivered to the mine. This was a difficult project with many technical issues. It had not been done before, but with the skill of the joint teams and cooperation of all, it was accomplished. It helped that the collaborating teams were located less than a mile apart.

As China's economy and industry grew (rapidly at that), the need for energy grew particularly for electrical energy. This was mainly from coal fired electric power plants. China has an abundance of coal mined from deep underground mines and open pit mines similar to the U.S.

China used much of the same mining technology as the U.S. Their open pit mines used large imported electric trucks and that ran inconsistent with their philosophy of making things themselves. But they did not have the technology to do so and because this technology was so difficult, they decided to obtain it from the U.S., the world leader at the time.

In 2011, they set up an electric truck engineering office to develop the technology and do the engineering design. They established the office in Detroit, Michigan where there were many vehicle engineers. However, the large electric truck engineers were in the western U.S. These engineers were busy with work in the western mines and had little desire to go to Detroit. So, the Chinese could not find qualified engineers to relocate to Detroit.

About that time, I received a call from one of the engineers from Reliance Electric who had worked on the development of the new electric trucks. He had been stationed in Tulsa, Oklahoma and retired there. He explained the work the Chinese were doing in Detroit with the electric truck and he and a group of our old team from Reliance had been hired by the Chinese. He had relocated to Detroit for the duration of the design work and they were paid very well. But they ran into some electric traction motor problems. They were importing the motors and they requested I travel to Detroit to discuss the problem and the possibility of consulting with them. I went to their Detroit office and determined that I could help them. Next, I met with the Chinese management. The meeting went well until I said I would come back with a contract for my consultation services.

I came back with a contract for my consultation work and reviewed it with the Chinese management. They thanked me for my offer and said they would get back to me in a week. I never received a response. So, I called my friend and he told me the Chinese do not do contracts because they do not like to be committed. I never went back. It was another long haul for no slide.

CHAPTER 17

CASE #15 INTERNATIONAL TRADE

The U.S. is one of the best places to do international business. It is the biggest and best market in the world. But equally important, it makes and meets its commitments. This begins with our tradition of a handshake to laws that enforce agreements. The U.S. is a country that meets the rule of law.

The Chinese do not make commitments that can be enforced by law. In China, a contract with a U.S. company is okay because it is doubtful the U.S. Company will be supported by law. However, if the business is in the U.S., both countries are supported by the law. In international trade it appears the U.S. has been the loser, starting with the North American Free Trade Association and going straight to the world trade agreements with China (which China has not met).

The Wall Street Journal reported on (August 29, 2015 in an article by David E. Sanger):

> "For two decades, American politicians have been escalating their rhetoric about how to confront a rising China, one that grabs territory in the South China Sea, vacuums up American jobs and mounts cyber attacks on the United States. But now both Republicans and Democrats face a different challenge: how to deal with a weakening China, whose behavior may be as aggressive as always, but whose faltering market poses an entirely different threat to American investors, companies and

workers – one that cannot be solved by sanctions, military build-ups in the Pacific and threats of retaliation"

This same article discussed Senator Marco Rubio's (Florida) and Govenor Scott Walker's (Wisconsin) tough talks on Beijing in foreign-policy, as U.S. markets have suffered following China's stock market crash. Rubio was reported to say,

> "The Chinese government's efforts to devalue its currency and global trade are a rising threat to our economic interests. China is a growing danger to our national security. We can no longer succumb to the illusion that more dialogue with China's current rulers will narrow the gap in values and interests that separates us."

Mr. Walker called this administration's response to Asia 'hollow'.

> 'This is the result: the Chinese are aggressively expanding their territory, building islands for military bases in the South China Sea. Beijing conducts massive cyber-attacks against the United States-stealing classified military data, stealing the personal information of millions of Americans, and stealing billions of dollars in intellectual property."

As shown previously, the Chinese do not meet their world trade commitments. Why doesn't the U.S. make the Chinese keep their promises or suffer the consequences of not following world trade commitments by taking away their World Trade Organization status?

We do not know why the U.S. does not take aggressive action but here are my thoughts:

1). Threat of war, either small wars or a major war, like World War III. The small wars are actually already happening in one small way or the other and the U.S. takes no action. A major war is doubtful as it is not in the interest of either the U.S. or China, at least in the short term. However, in the long-term, a major war

between the United States and China appears to be inevitable. Our conflicts of interest in the western Pacific area are too great. But this will happen when China is ready as China grows economically and militarily in power while the U.S. declines. China is determined to control the Asian Pacific and over time (unless the U.S. relinquishes its power) this will lead to a major war. This is a war the U.S. cannot win. It is too far away. If we could not conclusively win in North Korea and Vietnam, how could we win another war in the same area?
2). China is a major supplier to the U.S. and that is not to be disrupted. But, there is little the U.S. cannot make for itself. Especially with several million workers not presently employed. After all, most of the goods came from the U.S. in the first place. U.S. lumber is shipped to China to make furniture that is shipped back in a lower quality mode. There is too much of this cheap stuff needs and it needs to be improved or eliminated.
3). However, there is pressure on the U.S. government by U.S. businesses to not take away the source of cheap labor; but it is often not that cheap in overall business, as my case studies illustrate.

This is not political, as for years both the Republicans, the party of business and the Democrats, the party of the people, have not taken corrective action on this issue. The administration in 2008, told us it would correct the problem. It did not. In 2013, the administration made the same claim. And again, it did not remedy the situation. Yet, the goal of the party and of the people is to defend against the errors of business. Now, it appears that both parties respond to money. But, the Bible says "The love of money is the cause of evil." That we have!

It seems to be the nature of mankind for weaker entities to attempt improvement by external expansion instead of internal development. But often they are not strong enough to succeed and end up weaker. It is often stated "the only true growth is by internal development." Yes, many individuals seek to escape poverty by immigrating to a better place and in doing so improve their situation. That is the secret of America! But often, wealthy individuals risk their wealth in poorly orchestrated ventures and end up losing big. That is the basis of Capitalism. But, it must be done with great care and wisdom. Do not make an investment or take a risk you do not have to make if you cannot afford the consequences.

History is full of failed attempts of nations trying to improve by Imperialistic expansion. One good example is in Henry Kissinger's book *Diplomacy* where he states, "Hitler outlined the program of conquest of large tracts of land in Eastern Europe and the Soviet Union for colonization." Unfortunately, the Soviets refused to go along with German expansionism. This was a key factor in the defeat and total destruction of Germany in WW2. Germany was strong but not strong enough. Businesses fall into this same trap by attempting to improve through expanding globally instead of internal development. They often succeed when they are strong enough. But, businesses attempting to expand into China, they are often not strong enough.

The large investments made by American business into China have often made the U.S. business leaner. It also has made the U.S., as a nation, leaner. Somehow, despite being the strongest and richest nation in the world, the U.S. has incurred immense debt and cannot meet the U.S. social, civic and military needs. The U.S. market has become poorer with an influx of lower quality products. U.S. poverty has increased with the rise in unemployment resulting from so many poor trade agreements.

CHAPTER 18

JAPAN, INC.

In the late 1980's, the nation of Japan was often called "Japan Inc." due to its technical strength and because it operated as a national enterprise second only to the U.S. in economic size. It was thought that Japan would soon surpass the U.S.

Reliance Electric Company had a joint venture with the Ulvac Company in Japan. Ulvac was a world leading producer of high valcum products and systems as used in vacuum brazing to semiconductor vacuum deposition, which used variable speed drives. One of the Ulvac managers thought they should produce or own the electric drives and so he led the effort to obtain electric drives.

The joint venture between the two companies went very well. Some in Japan said it was the best USA-Japan venture to date. In the early 1980s, it was my good fortune to be a Reliance executive responsible for the joint venture business. In 1980, Exxon purchased Reliance. They left the above arrangement alone. The acquisition was contested by the U.S. government as they claimed it would be an antitrust conflict as Reliance's technology and Exxon's money would dominate the market. Reliance was to complete the Exxon development and then produce a revolutionary alternating current drive based on a unique inverter that Exxon had invented. This inverter would operate on 440 volt AC using transistors so the cost was low. At that time, transistors of that rating were limited to 220 volt devices, although it required twice as many – 12 versus 6. It was called the alternating current synthesizer (ACS).

To approve the acquisition, the government stated that the Reliance Drive Division was to be "Held Separate" from the rest of the Company that had responsibility for the ACS, which I was responsible for. This changed Reliance's business model known to be the industry leader. Reliance proceeded to complete the development with the Exxon engineers in New Jersey with the assignment of some of Reliance's best people. In the meantime, I worked with our Executive Vice President to work with the U.S. government in order to remove the 'Hold Separate" but after a few years and many meetings, we were not successful.

One evening as I surveyed one of my many trade magazines, I saw an advertisement from a sales company in Texas for 440 volt transistors at high ratings made in Japan. The next morning, I called the sales office in Texas and asked if they had these transistors. They said they did indeed so I asked if I might obtain a set to make an inverter, The Texas sales person asked me what I was doing the next day and if I would be able to accompany him to Japan. Two days later, we were in a small but very nice town in the middle of the Japanese Alps.

The following day, we went to the transistor plant and found ourselves in a room full of the plant staff. This unnerved me. I protested that all I wanted was sample transistors and just needed to talk to the 440 volt transistor engineer and did not need the whole plant staff. The engineer I needed to speak with was in attendance but all the others stayed as they "all were involved". So we proceeded to speak with the engineer whom I found to be the best. We obtained eighteen 440 volt transistors, enough for three inverters that we built in Cleveland – they passed all tests. This started a wonderful relationship resulting in one of our best suppliers for many years. I then understood what "all involved" meant. This meant the end of the ACS and killed the project as the 440 volt inverters were made with existing manufacturing technology.

Upon review, the U.S. government agreed to lift the "Hold Separate" and Reliance was whole again. My admiration for Japan was very high. Reliance made small inverters in three places: the US, Europe, and Japan. These were almost commodities with the only exception of 50 hertz versus 60 hertz. This caused conflict between the three areas which we resolved by having a "shot out" between them. They all greed and in one month were to provide quotes to me. In two weeks, the Japanese provided an excellent quote. A month later, Europe followed with a quote twice the price of Japan, and the U.S. was too busy to provide a quote at all. Japan did an excellent job of supplying the rest of the Reliance world for several years.

The above events increased my confidence in Japan, Inc. and in the possibility of Japan surpassing the U.S. As I worked with our joint venture, Reliance Japan Limited, as the U.S. executive, I gained more understanding. Each year I would travel to Japan and review with management the annual plan for the coming year. They would present a carefully worked plan that each year had 8% growth. I urged him to go for 10% but they did not agree, although they delivered 10%. So I approved his plan which was presented to the Board of Directors with the same result.

After the retirement of my primary contact within Ulvac, I worked with a new president and we followed the same process with the same result. However in early 1990 as the U.S. recession, I went to Japan with reservation as to their economy. This reservation increased when I learned that their incoming orders slowed. I am a firm believer in business cycles and it was time for Japan to be in the beginning of a slowdown. Shockingly, they presented an 8% growth plan. When I suggested a 4% plan, it was rejected as they would have to reduce costs which they did not want. I agreed to the 8% growth plan which was presented to the Board and obtained approval.

For the first time in history, their plan was not met and was in 'the red'. Japan, Inc. went into a slowdown that they have not yet recovered from. Japan is no longer believed to be on its way to surpassing the U.S. The reasons for this are many and beyond the scope of this book, but there are similarities with business in China. China is following the same path as Japan; a rapid rise followed by long-term decline. The moral is: unless the basic fundamentals are there the long-term prospects are not good.

Part Three: Conclusions and the Future

CHAPTER 19

Business Leadership

In the 1987 movie, <u>Wall Street</u>, actor Michael Douglas as Gordon Gekko, said "Greed is good." How did the U.S. get into this position? How did it get to where money dictates U.S. national policy?

An America based on freedom for all and a capitalist economic system was probably doomed to eventually reach this point. You can blame politics for letting the system get out of control. But, the people voted (or didn't vote) the politics into this position. Thomas Jefferson said, 'The government you elect is the government you deserve." Abe Lincoln said "Government of the people by the people". Despite noble goals we have let the system get out of control. We are killing the golden goose!

How do we correct this problem? It has been shown the government will not correct the problem and the people by themselves do not have the power (even if they wanted to correct the problem). What is needed is leadership! The only agent with the ability to solve this problem is business and its leaders.

I am reminded of a mid-sized U.S. company that produced machinery and was a leader in their field several years ago, receiving a large order for their product from China when the U.S. economy was in a rough spot. But, when the order reached the V.P. of Sales and Marketing, he rejected the order much to the consternation of all. His explanation was this would be the last order for this type of product from China as the Chinese would reverse engineer the design, make the product themselves, and sell it to the rest of the world. Therefore, there was no future for his company with this order. Since then, his company has progressed to now be the world leader in their product. He had took a short-term loss for a long-term gain.

Where are the business leaders of today with this kind of wisdom? There are a few but we must make many more. This starts with the U.S. business schools where the short-term profit focus must be changed to a more complete long-term view of the return of investment.

A new division general manager that I was assigned to several years ago asked me what my goal was as the engineering manager. I gave him the answer I thought he wanted. I said "My goal is to help the company make a profit." He then told me I was wrong and that the goal was to survive. With that direction, our company went on to become the leader in our field. He was right. We need more leaders like him now. The U.S. needs the birth of a "counter culture" where short-term gain is sacrificed for overall long-term gain. True business leadership is required for good management.

CHAPTER 20

AMERICAN IMPERIALISM

The present global imperialism might be said to have started in 1492 when Christopher Columbus discovered the Americas. This took capital from Spain, brains and brawn from the Portuguese, and sailing leadership from the Italians. Since it was capital from the Spanish Crown, the beneficiary was Spain. The mining and support labor was obtained free from the enslaved local labor, the gold went to Spain. This might be one of the largest returns on investment in world history. It's world free trade at its finest.

From this, Spain developed a global empire ranging from the Americas to the Philippines decimating the indigenous people as they went. In the 16th century, Spain became the mightiest empire in the world. In Spain, the gold was used for global expansion and internal consumption instead of internal development. What remains are magnificent cathedrals where dead saints can be worshiped. Spain is no longer a world power but a once mighty nation on the verge of present day financial collapse. Spain became weak.

The avoidance of foreign wars was mostly adhered to in the 19th century but the real change in course came from President William McKinley who started the United States on the course of American Imperialism.

The U.S. entered this era at the turn of the 19th century when in 1898 the battleship USS Maine was blown up and sunk into the Havana, Cuba harbor. It was blamed on Spain but never proven. It might have been an accident, but the press and the politicians blamed it on Spain and used it as an excuse to start a war with Spain and Cuba. This led to a war in the Philippines a few years later.

President Theodore Roosevelt led the way to American Imperialism and China. After the 1905 Japanese-Russian War, Roosevelt brokered a peace treaty for which he was awarded the Nobel Peace Prize. He got the Japanese to reduce their claims on Russia and in return, Japan received Korea which gave the U.S. a door to China for trade purposes – it was a "huge market".

He then dispatched a group of ships to tour Asia, a venture well described in James Bradley's book *The Imperial Cruise*.

> "In the summer of 1905, President Theodore Roosevelt dispatched the largest diplomatic mission in American history. Led by Secretary of War (and future president) William Howard Taft, the group traveled thousands of miles across the Pacific, docking in Hawaii, Japan, the Philippines, China, and Korea. Along for the ride was Teddy's daughter Alice, a media darling known for her wild behavior. She was not there by accident. Her father knew that Alice would be an effective distraction for the reporters covering the journey. And Roosevelt had very good reason to keep his true motives concealed. During this trip, Taft, on Roosevelt's behalf would negotiate a series of secret and wholly unconstitutional agreements that would lay the groundwork for America's Pacific engagement. These invisible treaties brokered with the sliver of Asians (whom Roosevelt deemed 'civilized' by virtue of their adoption of Western ways) would lead to World War II in the Pacific, the triumph of communism in China, the Korean War, and within decades, left tens of millions dead. The full details and implications of Roosevelt's illicit pacts would remain largely unknown until his own death, and then be effectively erased from the textbooks. "

In 1917, the U.S. entered into World War I followed by an isolationist period lasting until World War II. Again, the U.S. became imperialistic with the start of the Second World War providing most of the allied world with goods, materials and military throughout the world.

This time, imperialism stuck as the U.S. did not want to give up the gains made in World War II. As a result, we still have our military spread throughout the world.

Of course, the academic idealist especially espoused the idea of spreading democracy throughout the world. The U.S. business community loved the world market with cheap goods and cheap labor. They were both wrong. As the world does not want U.S. democracy and soldiers in their lands, the U.S. does not receive much of the expected return from its investment. Many are now recognizing this fallacy and trying to 'pull back'. But how do we do this? The path is simple. Get out of Asia. The execution of such a plan could and likely would be very difficult, but it is time for the us to 'bite the bullet'.

A few years ago, I accepted an assignment to conduct a business class at a major university in Bangkok, Thailand. This course was to instruct the students on the 'product development process' which starts with market research and progresses to technical viability, to product concept, to design, to manufacturing and finally, delivery to the market. This went well and I did it for two years. The students were in graduate school and were bright and hardworking. One day, the dean of the engineering school invited me to have lunch where we discussed a variety of subjects in addition to the course. I asked her what her purpose was in sponsoring the course. She explained they have to learn how to design and make products in Thailand themselves and not be subject to America using them for low-cost labor.

I then asked the dean what Thailand's position would be if the U.S. and China were to go to war. She immediately replied, telling me that they (Thailand) would have to support China. She continued that she loved Americans but Thailand's self-interests would best be served by supporting China because the U.S. was too far away to help Thailand. China is their 'next door' neighbor. It should be recognized that Thailand is a confluence of Chinese and Indian cultures with many of the people from either country.

That's the realism of our Asian 'friends'. The U.S. is loved, but we are too far away. They really want the U.S. capital and it is what they are getting. The real experience of the U.S. and Korea in the early 1950's and the Vietnam War in the 1960's proved this point. It's a lesson the

Asians remember well. In regard to all the good will and agreements between the U.S. and its Asian partners: the real politics say our Asian partners will side with China because they have to.

As the U.S. and China are already at war both economically and politically, it is highly probable that the course China is on will escalate into a military war the U.S. cannot win. The war will commence when China is ready and we will not be ready. It is not a war that the U.S. can win. It's not only too far away but China is building a modern military force while the U.S. is continuing to decrease its already overextended military. Our carrier navy which projects our power in the Far East is vulnerable compared to China's modern military.

But what about our allies and partners in Asia and the agreements we have made with them? It is best to stop deceiving them and start disengaging with our Asian allies as our promises cannot be met. This should start with a decrease in trade and progress to a decrease in military presence. Even if we could bring a military conflict to a close, the U.S. cannot afford such a conflict. The U.S. needs to invest its resources and technology internally because that's where the money and the future are. We need to rebuild our wealth which can be best done by focusing on internal development.

The present U.S. military arrangement in Asia is as good as our arrangement in the Middle East; the demands on human and material resources continue to worsen. The continuation of the U.S. imperialistic course will bring the U.S. to ruin. Our first priority is to avoid disaster or to survive. This priority is presently in jeopardy. Yes, it will be difficult to get out of Asia. It is always difficult to change an existing entrenchment but it must be done for the U.S. to survive. The hundred year old structure of American Imperialism is just as difficult to change. If it does not work for our benefit anymore than it must be changed. So if we know this change is needed, what's stopping it from happening? I believe it is because of special interest groups.

Key American businesses are the special interest groups taking capitalism to excess. Pope Francis, when visiting the U.S. on Sept 20, 2015, said on capitalism, "Uncontrolled it will devour everything that stands in its way of increasing profits." If businesses do not control themselves, it is to their own best interest, that the government must set aside its reluctance to control business.

I remember a quote I heard some time ago, "Success breeds its own failure". Capitalism throughout the world is successful at pursuing its goal of making a profit but it has been taken to the extreme and any extreme is breeding its own failure. Capitalism must be moderated. Is the government going to do it? No. Face that fact. It's supposed to and we elect them and they say they will, but once they get into office, they don't. The politicians seem to like that big business money.

It will only come if business management recognize that it is in their best interest to serve their American customers as their number one priority. After all, it's the customers that keep score. To do this, they must broaden their responsibilities to include not only long-term profit but the overall health of the company consisting of what we call stakeholders, customers, vendors, employees and a local community. When I first started working, the company I worked for did that. Most companies have abandoned that way of investing in the company as they send U.S. business to China.

CHAPTER 21

THE FUNDAMENTALS

The case studies presented in this book stand as examples of why doing business in China is not good business. Primarily, the business fundamentals are not satisfactory. My experiences in Asia, especially China, along with my research of existing literature have provided data for this opinion.

The total cost in China is higher than is generally thought, resulting in little or no cost advantage. But, do not confuse cost with price. Cost is fact, price is policy. China often presents a price lower than the costs but it is only temporary. Eventually a profit must be made or you will not have a good supply. After China has secured your business, they start the process of increasing price. When you will not tolerate any more price increases, they take out material in the product which cheapens the product to an unacceptable level.

There are distance and time zone differences that also contribute to the cost of conducting business with China. When delays occur in communication between the U.S. and China due to these differences, responses to market trends are slowed, causing a decrease in potential profit. Additionally, the expense of travel factors in.

Next, there is energy. In China, energy is in short supply making it an expensive commodity. Energy adds significant costs to the manufacture of a product. It also drives shipping and logistics costs. The cost of a quality product is high which is the reason products produced by the Chinese are often of unsatisfactory quality. This poor quality work then requires reworking or scrapping products to prevent the ultimate loss of the customer.

The basic costs are labor and material. Material is often the main cost, but most materials are globally priced, leaving China at no real advantage. In many cases, China must import at higher than world prices. Meanwhile, too often the decision to manufacture in China is based on their low labor costs. It is true the worker wages are much lower than U.S. wages, but that is only part of the cost of labor in China. There are significant add-on costs particularly high social costs. Furthermore, the Chinese labor costs have been and are increasing rapidly to where even labor cost is not an advantage.

The Chinese are eager to work but it takes considerable input and guidance from the U.S. to produce an acceptable product. This input is not only needed for the startup and transition but also in the mature phase of manufacture.

To further add to the situation, there is considerable labor unrest in China which makes labor management difficult and may ultimately drive the wages for workers in China higher. The U.S. Bureau of Labor indicated back in 2014, "This trend is showing a significant increase of wages versus the US, which will continue to decrease the advantage that China currently has over the US." That trend has continued on through to the present day.

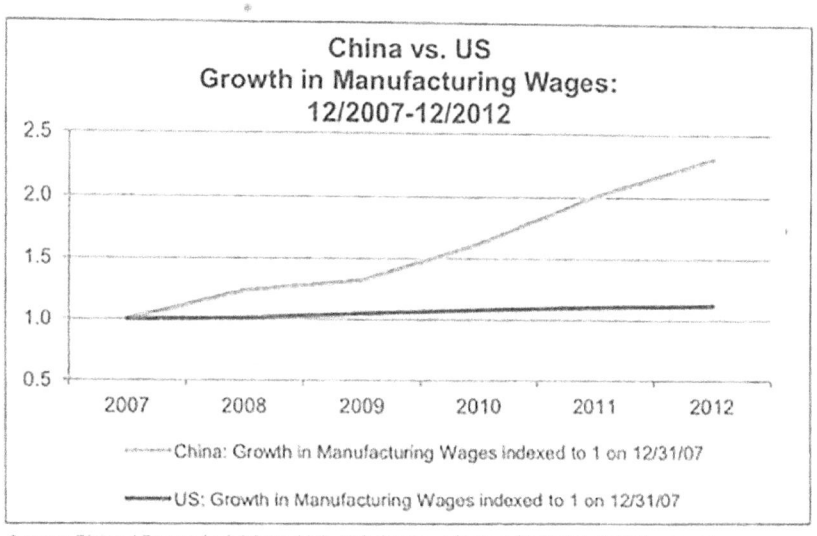

Source: Richard Bernstein Advisors LLC, U.S. Bureau of Labor Statistics, Nat'l Bureau of Statistics of China, Bloomberg

Finally, the 'old China hand' said, "Business in China is corrupt and predatory". But how did it get that way? China has a Buddhist ethic that teaches consideration and helpfulness to others. Then, the revolutions and wars of the first part of the 20th century severely eroded that ethic. The invasion by Japan from 1937 to 1945, the communist revolution and subsequent management by Mao until almost 1970 destroyed China. A poor, troubled country to start, the people suffered more than any other country.

John K. Fairbank, a noted China historian wrote: "Public spirit, generosity and even honesty were more than most people could afford. The strong not only trampled on the weak, they gouged one another."

Add to the above, the traditional communist ethic and practice as seen in Europe and you have a difficult place to work. The values and goals of communism are different than American democracy. China is full of complexities which the U.S. decision makers are often ignorant of and have a limited perspective on. Considerable difficulty is encountered in trying to overcome the above fundamental discrepancies. This adds up to the conclusion that conducting business in China is a poor business decision.

CHAPTER 22

The Future

It is commonly thought that China has the largest manufacturing base but lags behind the West in invention. Their manufacturing has grown by mainly taking products and technology from the West and selling it back at lower prices. Along the way, they have often added worthwhile innovations which I define as a novelty that can be made and sold at a profit. However, this should not be confused with invention, which is more basic and can fuel the future.

The Industrial Revolution started with the United Kingdom and traveled to the U.S., giving the West the lead on considerable innovation but also much invention. Consider the steam engine, the internal combustion engine, the electric motor, and electronics all the way from vacuum tubes to the semiconductor-based computers and information technology. It is questionable if progress can be made without invention. Currently, China is behind the West in invention. This is not a generic claim though, as many of the leaders of invention in the West are Asians, and China has a history of invention as well. Consider gun powder and for the greater good, the invention of paper as we know it - both are from China. Therefore it must be the system.

One of the most important inventions in the history of mankind was writing. But, for thousands of years, it was limited to stone and clay which were hard to duplicate. This changed with the invention of paper as we know it. While the Egyptians first produced a form of paper from a papyrus plant, the existence of paper from tree pulp began in China in about 100 BC This significantly reduced the time and cost of communication with words and pictures. Many centuries later, the invention of the Gutenberg printing press in Western Europe made information available to the masses which enlisted their energy to create progress. Today information is transmitted at the speed of light throughout the world by electronic technology employed by China but obtained from the West.

Why is China now lagging in invention? It might be the Chinese military control of information and the Communistic dictatorship system. Add to this the civil unrest with over 100,000 active rebellions in China each year, making China's future as a leader unclear. Although China is rapidly building physical structures for science, scientific progress and invention need more than a physical structure. It needs an open mindset and freedom of individual action and group interaction. The Chinese communist dictatorship does not permit this. China will have a difficult future, one not good for investment and business.

The future financial integrity of China also poses a risk to investment. "China debt levels have soared. Overall debt has increased to about 250% of GDP, up from 150% six years ago. The key factor is state control of the financial system." (Taken from an article in *Economist*, 10/15/2014)

We need to learn from the past to assure the future. In the early 19th century, the UK was a leader in technology and applied that to transportation, civil infrastructure, military and other areas such as manufacturing. At that time, the UK was a mediocre nation, but with that focus, it was able to produce products of value and begin global exportation. This created immense wealth and by mid-century the UK was a leading nation. They even colonized some of their international customers which required a strong military, especially navy, to maintain which the UK could afford. They became Imperialistic. This worked so well the UK focused on world trade at the sacrifice of internal development. They thought this was an easier way to create wealth. By the end of the 19th century, the UK was in decline and their economic and military strength was less than perceived as well. Their decline has continued to this day exacerbated by the loss of their colonies, World War I and World War II.

In the same time period, Germany has gone from a loose collection of kingdoms to a united nation. By mid-19th century with focus on internal development and investment in the future, Germany pushed through WWI, WWII, hyperinflation, depression and integration of East Germany to become a great nation. This is the "German way."

What about the future of the United States? Some say it will be equally poor with many economic, human, military and civil issues. As an optimist, I reject that scenario because the great human and material resources of the U.S. will overcome those (and other) issues to become the leading nation (again) by the end of the century. However, as a realist, I accept the issues are real and unless they are managed well, the potential of the U.S. will not be reached. In less than fifty years, from a monetary point of view, the U.S. has gone from one of the richest nations to one of the poorest as measured by national debt. Many say this is not a problem as the U.S. can print more money as needed. Of course that decreases the value of the dollar even if it may stave off bankruptcy. Never mind the wealthy 1% of the population and that the stock market keeps growing. These are not good measures of the nation's real wealth.

Let's look at the bottom of the ladder. From 1959 to 1966, the number of people in the U.S. living below the poverty line had fallen from 22.4% to 14.7%. That's a real creation of wealth. It continued to fall to 11% but then it started climbing and by 2012 it was back up to 15%. This means that almost 50 million people in the United States are poor. That's not wealth! I do not want to debate the effect of social programs on the increase of poverty. I believe the root cause of the lack of a generation of wealth is due to the transfer of manufacturing to other nations, particularly China. This results not only in loss of U.S. revenues but a loss of jobs as well, leaving the number of unemployed at a record high.

I believe U.S. businesses are responsible for more than just a return on short term profits which makes a few people very rich and encourages the stock markets to grow. U.S. businesses are also responsible for protecting the present U.S. markets to insure their future. The financial squeeze also forces a decrease in the U.S. national security which makes the U.S. more vulnerable to harm, increasing the risks for U.S. businesses to operate off shore. This results in the decrease of the U.S. market and the source of good revenues for U.S. business. Bad business due to bad management!

About 30 years ago, the U.S. was enjoying a strong economy. Actions were being taken to reduce inflation and employment was good. At the same time, most of China was in abject poverty. There was a glut of people with too few jobs, for the communist plan was not working. However, there were many people who would work hard for many hours at low wages. The Chinese government instituted the 'One Child per Family' law to keep the population in check. They also decided to market to the U.S. and get some of their wealth. This was not capitalism, as the communist government was still in tight control. This worked for the Chinese as millions of people were lifted out of poverty and a large middle class was created.

In the same period in the U.S., the U.S. working class had seen their inflation-adjusted income decrease while living costs increased as the middle class was destroyed. As a result, unemployment had increased. The unemployment rate would grow to about 11% - very high! Debt had reached unsustainable levels with service cost one of the highest items in the budget, keeping taxes up. That was bad news for the U.S. It's about as bad as it will get though, and in time it will improve. Jobs are coming back to America.

China now has a shortage of labor and has implemented a two-child family. This will take years, to give them a labor edge once again, if it ever does. To decrease prices of their product, China has reduced the value of their currency, which is a good way to go broke. The real value of a U.S. investment in China has decreased. The U.S. has a great future! All that is needed is good leadership from the business leaders, not the government. If the U.S. can return to practical and wise leaders in business, our future will be great! Our dollar has increased to high values and we are on the way to a solid economy.

CHAPTER 23

CONCLUSION

The evidence presented shows investing in China is not good business. At the least, the return on investment is probably negative. The principle is also at risk and the base business might be lost or end up in China's courts. The purpose of management is to obtain a return on investment. This also means the return of capital principle. Therefore, it must be bad management to invest in China. Why then would very bright, highly educated people invest in China even at the risk of losing the business?

China is a large power house with many attractions for investors. It is a huge market with low costs. Many managers see this as the solution to the low growth and return on their U.S. business. But these attractions in China are not available to outsiders on a sustaining basis. China wants to own all the businesses in China. China is for the Chinese! That is what the Chinese government and the people want, and the U.S. cannot change their plan.

So, with an inadequate analysis and lack of knowledge, businesses go to China seeking large gains. This is not good management. The real solution to their domestic business problems lies in the modernization of their U.S. business, in the sales, marketing, product development, plants, engineering and their management of people and processes. Joseph Schumpeter, Economist and Political Scientist once stated, "Destruction is a mechanism for progress."

We must reexamine the responsibility of modern management. In our capitalistic system the main responsibility is still to obtain a return on investment. The total time frame must also be considered in both short term and long term perspectives. It appears much of today's management focuses on the short term. Often, this happens at the sacrifice of the long term and the overall health of the business. This depends on both the internal operations and the market served. Internal operations require constant effort as does the market served. But, wisdom is needed for the market decisions. The main purpose of marketing is to find the right market. This needs knowledge of the markets and business wisdom not acquired in schools alone but rather through business experience. Here in lies the modern American tragedy. The U.S. is the richest market in the world but is being sacrificed in the faulty pursuit of short term gains in a larger market we know little about. Even after much effort, this results in decreased return on investment. This is bad management.

It seems to be the nature of mankind for weaker entities to attempt improvement by external expansion instead of internal development. But often, they are not strong enough to succeed and end up weaker. It is often stated "The only true growth is by internal development". This is the basis of capitalism – it must be done with great care and wisdom. Do not make an investment or take a risk you do not have to make if you cannot afford the consequences. Businesses that understand this and have stayed with the U.S. market while investing in their U.S. operations have seen better results. This is good management.

Julie Makinen and Chuan Xu from the Los Angeles Times, in Beijing, China, January 21, 2016 recorded,

> "More than three-fourths of American companies in China feel less welcome than in the past, and 45 percent say revenue is falling or flat, a survey released Wednesday by the American Chamber of Commerce in China found."

Much has been written on the decrease of American growth over the past 30 years. There are books full of data with a diversity of reasons for the decline. Another approach is to start with a few fundamentals such as the 'law of supply and demand' coupled with 'necessity is the mother of invention.' From World War II the demands for materials and labor caused a shortage that continued from the 1950's into the 1970's as the world was dependent on the U.S. for goods and materials. U.S. labor was in short supply and good jobs with good pay became available. Businesses were profitable and funded innovation which further created products the world wanted.

But this changed with the input of one billion new Asian workers into the world labor supply. This created a surplus of U.S. labor and a decrease in good jobs that continues to this day. As labor was outsourced, the profits went with it and business could no longer support the development, further decreasing U.S. competitiveness. This resulted in a decrease in social services and a large increase in debt. With the increase in population control and world labor supply coupled with internal consumption, the total world labor excess is decreasing. This means more U.S. jobs will be createdas the labor shortage is being corrected. U.S. growth will resume!

The key is to encourage the once prized intelligence and leadership of U.S. business management where the measure of a person was in the 'quality of their work and the quality of their character'. What is the measure of U.S. business leadership today? Is it leading or is it lacking?

Acknowledgements

It was fortunate, I did not know how difficult it would be to write a book about my knowledge and involvement in China because I may not have started it. My biggest obstacle was that the reader may confuse this manuscript as a dissertation in Chinese-American Economics. It was not my intent to give mathematical proofs for the claims I have presented. This book is a compilation of my ideas and opinions based on over sixty years of professional business experience including international responsibility frequently involving China.

Sixteen cases are presented as testimony that support the conclusions that are made. This is my disclaimer. This manuscript is not meant to cause harm to any person or company although errors among some have been identified. My hope is that this book will aid those involved in managing U.S. businesses as they try to overcome the critical challenges of effectively dealing with China and attempt to understand what can realistically be achieved.

I very much appreciate the kind, thoughtful words of John Mueller in the Foreward of this book. It is true that my "long and varied career had exposed (me) to every facet" and that encouraged me to keep writing the story of the business we did in China.

Also, I am thankful for Mike Middletown from Bluffton Motor Works because he introduced me to China after accompanying me on several early trips there. He was the best way to understand conducting business there as we worked together for many years.

My talented daughter, Diane Dynes, has labored numerous hours editing and keeping track of the many drafts of this manuscript produced over the past three years. I am most grateful that she has promoted my written stories as "data with a soul ... that need to be told" and because of that, these words have been put to print.

About the Author

Peter J. Tsivitse graduated from the Case Institute of Technology in 1952 with a Bachelor of Science in Electrical Engineering. He then started work as a Motor and Control Design Engineer with Reliance Electric & Engineering Company. In addition to his career with Reliance Electric, Dr. Tsivitse served in the United States Army with an overseas assignment. He used the Korean War G.I. Bill to obtain his M.S. and Ph.D. from Case Institute while he was employed by Reliance Electric & Engineering Company.

Reliance Electric was founded in 1904 as a producer of mechanically adjustable speed D.C. electric motors for machine tool drives. By 1925, the company was producing electrically adjustable speed drives with an AC to DC motor-generator power source and magnetic controls in a packaged drive. By World War II, it used tube-based electronic control. In 1960, it used solid-state control and power source. Soon after it employed computer control serving the drive product market, as well as, drive systems in major industries such as steel and paper. Reliance became the major producer of electric motors both AC and DC in World War II for the U.S. Navy. Afterwards, Reliance made acquisitions in the electric motors and mechanical power transmission. In addition, Reliance diversified with the purchase of Toledo Scale Company and the communications industry. In 1979, Exxon purchased Reliance. By 1985, Reliance management purchased the company through an LBO and an initial public offering. In 1995, the company was bought by Rockwell

International. At that time, Reliance Electric products were leading brands and return on the investment was excellent.

Dr. Tsivitse lived through this time period as he progressed from Design Engineer to Engineering Management, Plant Management, Operating Vice President and eventually Corporate Vice President until his retirement in 1995. Following retirement, Dr. Tsivitse has served as a consultant to a large variety of industries and companies in product design and business development.

NOTES

1. The Art of War by Sun Tzu: an ancient Chinese military treatise, 5th Century BC

2. Spectrum North America, January, 2016

3. Jack Welch and Leadership: Executive Lessons of a Master CEO by James W. Roberson, October 23, 2001

4. Advance in Superconductivity, New York Times, December 14, 2007

5. Chinese Firm is Charged in Theft of Turbine Software by Mathew L. Wald, New York Times, June 27, 2013

6. The Great Brain Robbery, 60 Minutes segment on NBC, January 17, 2016

7. The Wall Street Journal, August 29, 2015

8. Diplomacy by Henry Kissinger, Touchstone Books, April 4, 1995

9. Wall Street: Money Never Sleeps, 20th Century Fox, 2010

10. The Imperial Cruise: A Secret History of Empire and War by James Bradley, Back Bay Books, November 8, 2010

11. Full Text of Pope Francis' Remarks to Congress, by Larisa Epatko, PBS Newshour, September 24, 2015.

12. Why Success Often Breeds Failure, by Greg Satell, Forbes Magazine, November 1, 2013.

13. U.S. Bureau of Labor Statistics, Nat'l Bureau of Statistics of China, Bloomberg, Richard Bernstein Advisors LLC, 2014

14. Chinese Debt: A Moral Deficit, Economist, October 15, 2014

www.ingramcontent.com/pod-product-compliance
Lightning Source LLC
Chambersburg PA
CBHW061443180526

45170CB00004B/1531